SORRY WAS IN THE WOODS

SORRY WAS IN THE WOODS

MICHELLE TARANSKY

OMNIDAWN PUBLISHING
RICHMOND, CALIFORNIA
2013

Cover art:
"Civil Settlement" by Richard Taransky, FAAR '00,
Artist in Residence '05 with The Fabric Workshop and Museum,
Philadelphia, PA.

Interior images by Richard Taransky:
"Bath House""Bride's House""Cinema"
"City Gate""Exit Section""Grand Stands""House"

Book cover and interior design by Cassandra Smith

MIX
Paper from
responsible sources

FSC
www.fsc.org

FSC® C092540

Cataloguing-in-Publication Data is available from the Library of Congress.

Published by Omnidawn Publishing, Richmond, California
www.omnidawn.com   (510) 237-5472   (800) 792-4957
10 9 8 7 6 5 4 3 2 1
ISBN: 987-1-890-650-81-0

table of contents

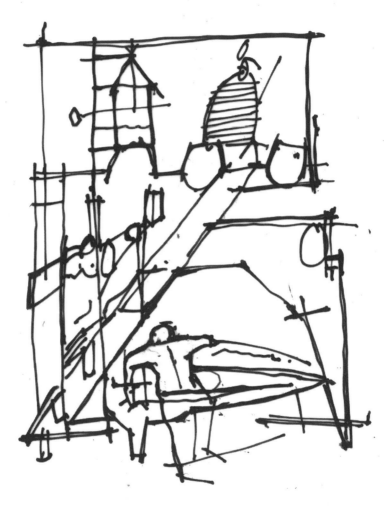

SORRY WAS IN THE WOODS

when changing woods means changing woodsmen

there isn't a woodsman to say stop

saying that is a symbol for that thing

another who may stop another reason why

you feel anxious when you mean timber

or their refusal to name the specific place

when to stop when to insist it is time

to say you are a question in the collapse

so leave the woods so the woods becomes there

where it's too much a raised voice raising

confusion between threats and pointing

to the alleged plan I decided to make

the choices I do a disorder that prevents

a productive fall despite another woodsman leaving

like the exact fire you imagined I said whisperdanger

said I admit fault and I cannot say it again

in another woods of preferences where someone

will of course choose to separate the panic

disorder from the panic when the wind is an explorer

with closed eyes you focus on worrying the witness will be

so scared he'll cry out not scary not for those who prefer the woods

never be able to approximate the fall the woodsmen can

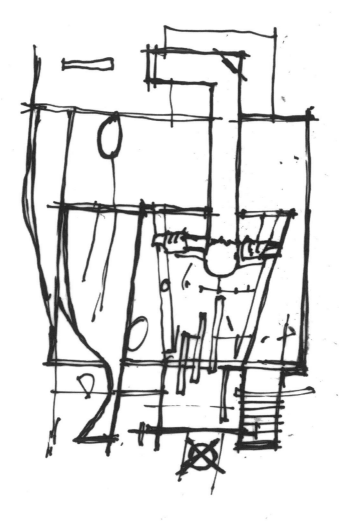

THE NECESSITY OF A LINE OR A WORK TO BE AS WOODS IS, TO BE AS CLEAN AS WOOD IS AS IT ISSUES FROM THE HAND OF NATURE, TO BE AS SHAPED AS WOOD CAN BE WHEN A MAN HAS HAD HIS HAND TO IT.

Charles Olson

WHEN THE WOODS IS WHERE

We came out here
to figure out figuring
out— Which woods took
what tree from the bodger
made symptoms
into a sentence
to harbor your feverfew
ideas about chances
and their damage
when it comes to

You are preaching at the timber beasts.

After figuring it all out
before admitting you were
told about the working conditions
outside the window— That its cracks
were, as well, the people you see
you look like a wolf. A mistake
to say you are a history
a more current idea
concerning how to move
from the city
center. We figure
out the way to conquer
by conquering. That
the lumberman is a lumberman
instead of a logger
is written in the manual
if only you were
looking, for excuses
not to change directions

HOW TO PICTURE THIS PLACE WHERE

Ash is strong and looks
Like chestnut— A tree is like a steer.
There are many kinds of cuts. Gentle polishing
Exposing the figure of the wood.
You will be surprised when you place
Light wood in hot sand. Watch the wood
Slowly burn. Refinish a found chair
To appear new.

NO, I WILL BE IN THE WOODS

Carving a term

Onto the already sick
Tree with the right

To make it look the same

As the door
Frame between our house

And not our house where
The bodgers are meant

To pass through what other reason

Would there be to build
It? Address it

As if there is no other

Way to find
The need in the felled

Here to defend every failed pastoral
Story you invented

SORRY IN THE WOODS WHERE

I am looking for a language
With a word that means
We must see it all
Differently: the accounting
For their symptoms
When we are calling it a day
Using the wage to mark
Our place as the place
That makes crimes
Build an own shelter
Out of arguments
Facing past

KNOW I WILL BE IN THE WOODS

Waiting at the gate for you

To fall having already forgotten

How you swore the sentence

Was meant to

Be joined with

That sentence. The yes

One. It responds to your

First question. Why are we given

The tools for fixing the old

House we thought was

Keeping our best ideas

In its doorways.

A way to watch the clock

In a room without

A clock or daylight

To draw accurate shadows. Shadows

That are thinking what you are

Thinking. How to call me

Into question.

THE PLANS CAUTION

Was should, was a foundling was the truth was it was found as they found it
to hold their gaze in place of a sanctuary, a ruin of many sanctuaries one signal
for being too close to the admonitioner carrying news of the collecting tales
like they are evidence like the uniformed watching the trying current once lost
then the chance storm, turn, declaration goes disappearing and foregrounds
collision with chorus— if we say it all at once this ground can say it turns its ash
to measure where measure is a burning axe & that they follow them

IN THE SEVEN WOODS

We have a machine

We cannot explain

Why watching the event

We making all facts be one fact

To watch parents

Watch their parents

Mount a rebellion

A THOUGHT THE SAME AS THE BOUGH

The rules our tree has found are already

A story that is about trees carved from houses

This rain will not worry the housekeeper

The rules are a stairwell and a series of revolving doors

Do not look towards the staring neighbor

Plan for figuring for facing echo of later

Overstating the work. Where

It's the piece of the tree growing symbolic, if you let them

Expect woodpeckers to be plastic and panicking from

Sorry, the carpenter is not a painter of the forest.

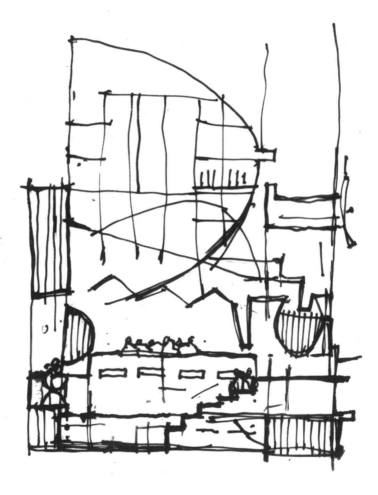

—YOU'VE GOT TO BE CAREFUL IN WOODS

Louis Zukofsky

THE PLANS CAUTION

sorry wasn't

watching or a note

needed to remember

parents move out of their

houses and the watcher will see

the first figure

estimating the line between a wood-

land and getting

a made table

to be then

a house, the house

holding what it is

made out of

it is all four of those

the landgrabber once

warned the workers to caution because of the separated dwelling
song and the certainty and the fact is, it turned it fails it sees the chair
as there as waiting for the work to assume the work's place, the plan
called Every Century

a war that closes

like a door

you have been made

to face— to sit at a table to prove the proposition, when repeated then heard only entrance, entrance and difference catching itself in the spine then entrance is what they say is evidence of the disagreement charged as though that is common

it's not the bodger there instead it's

about what work was

bodged & why the plan called

for separate constructions

and had them

built—   what lies over walls

figures gone

WILL GO NORTH THROUGH WOODS TO THE WOOD

Will see a tree farm as a woods

What is on the easel

Where my father is working

Before the subject

Two trees of the same age

Burning on a woodburning stove

We speak of the keeping of the woods

As we would of the keeping of a picture

Of a light in a place without trees

He never learned how to

Properly pose with an ailing wood

Despite the index of common tree diseases

Who is prepared for disease

To spread from tree to tree

To make a series of choices

They matter to the woodsman

Even though he lives in a forest

He does not waste firewood

THE PLANS CAUTION

Figure themselves

Saying itself

Won out

After land

Scape to hold

The entire thing up to

Itself without echo

A gate opening to
A room for
A room with
A room not
A room of
A room was
Put to flame
To have the worriers stop it

Waiting since

Their positions are their

Answer—

Yes, it is what my father built

And is not

IF THIS IS A GOAT, I WILL TELL YOU

The goat is used as an insult
With a wide range of meanings
You said the best reason
An answer with a reference
When you mark breaths
As if loss and land use may escape
Calculation or revenge
Like naming the woods after the river
I wanted to begin differently

THE PLANS CAUTION

Ruin of the sum
Their builders didn't draw on

Windows like the coffin
Setting up the site

Like a house
Was black, smoke and an act

Too many trees wanting to be like bodies

The table-
Leg's shadow on your leg

They meant no-altar
Let this altar be the only thing raised

At the confession where daughter is a mirror the son is a grave that
cannot hide a hole in the roof that is emulating botched work, the
sawhorse, the neverchair, the time clock he didn't clock out

It's ticking— that they can understand
It can't be five, he

Always comes to the table then

DESPITE THE WOODS

This is a novel
Reciting disease
After disease after
Spending the season
At a stranger's place
Wood-evil halting— I

Take it broken
Teach cruelty to the home
Why using thresholds why
It doesn't matter who knows
Who forgave who for taking

The doors from the plans
Reason why you are the whale
Here not in the work but
The plan for another
Picture where we are

Wolvewhales and sheepwhales
You could be the woodcut
Cut into the wood
That sounds like worship
Stops like

Stop saying beautiful things
I'm worried about losing
The house this whole
Fall when
Starts from scratch
The scratch

THE PLANS CAUTION

A botched job

The job that proved

Necessary to be done

The bones of this

Sleeping next to

Stranger in spring

His boy singing if

Only a door had

A hall, a halting

Way to be being

Fitted while talking

With shadows— They are

Falling look they

Won't be examples or failures, won't be

Where when we finish them

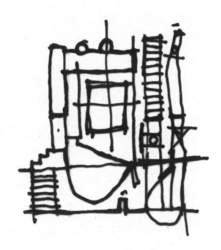

THE LEAVES ARE FALLING. POINT THINGS OUT.
PICK UP THE RIGHT THINGS.

Bob Perelman

DO NOT THINK TIMBER

Do not think timber. Think I

Only when thinking I am a faller
Among fallers— Here it is neighboring

To keep the wolves
From the door

Where we see war know war increases their

Need for wood
Thinking fire then the misplaced records
We need for the facts to place the blame
Where it belongs

They will tell you the reason

When they say that gesture
Is called waving, I say, no
No, she is reaching out

To create the correct comparison
To war time we look like the son
Looking to the window seeing

Only the window say
Only the window
Is a threshold

Whose practice
Is bodies you insist will equal
The statement about

Most people make the mistake
And call the work a craft. You know
A craft when you are on it on the way
To

Groundwork. It is still important
To prepare
The surface of the woods
Before finishing

Do not turn on me
In front of them

A PROPOSAL FOR A CLEARING

A clearing wherein they would
Share a ransom note

With the front line's sorrow
Song in its moment. The first
To cross the measured

Strut without eyes
Without saying another
Model—   That alleged pair

We fear will
Take out
A loan like the blind are

A sinking war
Knew the planner's
Playing a builder at a border town

Saw ballads as armed
Forces— The division from said
To lost perspective, its
Accusing lines

They are both in the same sentence here
It is a war see no one
Keeps writing

Here what figures are are
Steel and they
Are in need of

Woodsmen they are
Proposing they
Name a copy
After a copy

That went yellow

As was
Indicated by its caption

It's built nothing
Like they are

WHEN *IS* IS NOT THE

question behind loss
replacing the effect
concerned with support
what she says the work
is all about— a thing
being a being. our own
that we don't own it

STRANGER IS NOT THE PARTICULAR

To describe how neighbor looks

Like he was planning an exit

Yesterday— Told you to stand in the doorframe

For scale. Act as if you are not nervous. I have

This on tape do not ask me to feel like

I am not in a bad place there. I arrived

On time and holding a woods. The trees were

Boats here. Familiar with the properly described

Maps for fears, a key towards explaining

A bank run in terms of progress

The belief he reasons in the woods' favor

Whisper in another voice what

If he is not willing to pay

Attention. And this is a victory.

No questions. Going down the river.

BLOOD BANK

where else would you expect
the collection to be connected to
the way the holder struggles with the
want to hold back explaining

one can only run back to the other
so many times before saying I see blind
sums instead of an empty account
where your memory is the same

as what is happening behind locked doors
that isn't about what they would say
had they known you were the one
counting this deciding what to consider
enough

BLOOD BANK

Why would I have
Chosen to be angry
With them when others'
Wages were at stake
A bloodline, a wolfsound
The where as a lower limit
Cough indistinguishable from cry
Crying there is sick there waiting
The methods promising the clear
And just one more crime to prepare
There— This particular
Time you aren't there

A PROPOSAL FOR A CLEARING

Hunting for the shape you counted on me to look into trading plans for places as undoing had happened, happened on the banished ones— I trapped their breath and hoped it would turn into your handout because hiding the roots does not do enough we will say this they said that

.

We can't talk about it because it
Uses a figure
You said you saw
Places I saw no place
For their dying
Bird stories
He told he had
To cross a number of

Doors like a storm
Door and the door he lets go
Goes you will know what to call it by the shape you will know nothing like them disaster them houses passing through a house that can not capture a wolf where we were promised in a note of glass they were there waiting for an opposite to what injured drawing-room to house the current news where nothing has been

Planned— To think fallout,
The choice, the limits shared, and then

The question of which pronoun
Until you

Read the work, don't find it
A reflection, find
He has not
Built anything
He has planned

STOP! I DID NOT DRAG MY FATHER BEYOND THIS TREE.

Gertrude Stein

FOR DAYS I HAVE NO IDEAS

what worrying identifies the failed procedures from your letter that
never intended to invent the confession that the window was there
where I have not been recording falls that can measure the smallest
amount of light to be recommended to write by while being careful
what is visible when the first meeting is another language another
attempt to mean to leave space for your ideas nothing is a sentence is
it a line leading to a safe that was there until then you are nearer the
relationship between them and theirs I said the account is overdrawn
I meant the results remain unpredictable despite the extra room
and increased daylight when this is aftershock what happened to
the celebration the phone call to explain how to reintroduce figures
without a different process of checking your work the sum to prove and
ruin the idea about sums no patience for exchange between currencies
who share a country the order to hand over my share of the property

SORRY ASKED TO

Complete the work
To travel to the woods
They have abandoned

Your favorite details
Distinguished from the fire

Parts of burning
Burning the neighbor

And the neighbor is guest
Who is a messenger who is

A large house with windows for doors
I am going to the woods

And I am nightward
The night is waiting

To say it more than
You are asked to

To call the way to the woods
The main woods the settled

Woods a woods that were
A smaller place than now

The pacing is that practice
Landing the forest onto the field

Children in the woods by the pond
Measuring the breadth by their bodies

One crying in this wilderness

THE PLANS CAUTION

It replaces it repairs the parents their preference for room to work in, their
Preparations that keep adding a room that is a river, isn't that another
Room, another river that will be followed like a different sound
Another making it

Your work could be running from a room to an other
Room to find the gatekeeper who lies
In the doorway awaiting the wolf who cries

Entering is and entering
Crying wolf— I know you are
Here I said here
It is at the door

It knows me like I know it
A stand in for what spells

What spaces are concerned with the syllable, the scared of what
Standing in for they and their conditions wanting nothing

What was brought along
We didn't have

To introduce
There

The amassing
Sentences are
What built it

What describes the resulting
Image that is
Two images:

It is not a cabinet

Where one may be hidden

SORRY WAITING FOR THE

Permission to consider the view
They left me in their house

Looking like a false alarm. It was then
A fire went unnoticed. I call to see

If the woods is not the world.
Tell me, *We cannot picture any worse*

Fall. A hundred and four
Years ago, the woodcutter met

A description of how much they can
Tolerate. Sentences that are not told

Apart from those including: *Do you know the author?*
This is a known picture of that tree.

Worry. The injury was hard on me,
Too, it was. Far too quiet to ask

Questions. They have the whole book
Or nothing. We are counting

Against the grain. We are addicted
To evidence

WAITING FOR THE BODGER

To approach the tribute previously forbidden

To ask permission

Because you repeat it twenty times

It doesn't mean it happened

Twenty times. How I work

With my surroundings

The particular insistence

I don't know I can't

Even remember. Leaving

Places being ashamed for you

Afraid of suggesting work

In the face of reflection

This is written in a frame

That is too small

FOR DAYS I HAVE NO IDEA

the house is in the warehouse the flowers on the wrong tree a manual
in need of repair the remaining meat not yet being made have no idea
how the blind in the inlay assembly line a tree cut with a miniature axe
the father demanding it the records demanding like the misunderstood
a sum in the archive the archive in the house afraid of the calculation in
the prayer book the reminder if you see him say I say it's been days

THE DIFFICULTY OF DESCRIBING TREES

for the reason not unlike your
border between you from your
projections

the proper mode of address
you have used to understand
landscapes we call last
or late— don't read
what is left to invade
if not a watcher, a wolf
having wind that be
the beggar: forget how
the search ended for who is held
responsible has seen an outcry
in the woods

SORRY HID IN THE

Woods like the woods
is the last workaround.
How to define an approach
after an approach

that changes. The current
and its anticipation
circling the clamor clamor
to await a witness and his
dictionary: both a cross
made from the particular
trees sold by dividing
chair and axe
into ash

building the woods
from a description

SORRY WANT TO KNOW

want to know who will
struggle they called it a win
cough a report cough that
there are splinters before
ending in the singular being
misheard all trusts for waiting
waiting there we are coming to yell
into the kindle the questionable
the same equation— this faller did
push the roof out make a window
hold frame for what says
it's a sentence is writing the way the struggles
repeating we are a fever
we are against the door
waiting to be figured
waiting to be confused
who meant to ask who took the credit
for the work for the note where
you say I started to blame
you say you coughed on will
say please
know there was waiting
was an event before the event
gasped no forest, no wood, yet,
you've built a boat where no way
fails to shadow
what opposes

YOU WILL WATCH PEOPLE BEING SENTENCED

Like the week I planned
To keep a daybook
To keep it quiet
In the room of our place
We haven't seen lately
But from those perspectives
We expected a paragraph
In light of the fall

FROM THE WOODS, THE SOUND

has need to demand a promise be said before the river you took to
take the place the plan of where we will meet at the end of the season
to adjust our predictions, say the water, it carries, what it can and yes
this is that river and this is that river we are in it the woods you say they
keep you looking for the last sings the bird

THE PLANS CAUTION

Through the falling and not fallen threshold they will

Come at themselves passing into a building but it not being there

There when the news broke there a machine was there for identifying a log

With no purpose to be held up to the last name was not a name to be planned

Around. Its calling caused the father to have

Had tears— Coming down his face not wanting

To see his face waiting for his son to pass

FEAR, IN THE WOODS

You can teach your child
Fear. In the woods

That child can come to

Know there is a debate there

I'm saying it's appropriate

To begin explaining and please
Don't worry

The terms are wrong
The furniture is in the house
Like it is no different than

Forests you can't imagine
Feeling badly about

The feelings if they get into an
Argument where I am repeating:

If I cannot make you agree
Why write to you. If we will not

Begin with common place

Because it correlates it does
Not accept the premise
At that point that is the we
Where our poor bleeding son
Keeps calling this a storm
Calling out the fact as facts

To no bodger agreeing to listen

For the gunman looking for them

To help with the symptoms
Leading to the worst fever

Written about in the fear book

On the date of the incident,

Your diagnosis makes me identify them

& what can we do with the they
To disrupt them

Point to examples.
Stop or I will make it known

What the audience wants
The audience to know more

Talk about both: how they listened
For what moved people

AFTER THE TIMBER THE

harm was caused
already— there also was
made up of neighbor who
is othering habits they
have no scars to trace
even looking in a mirror
no scars or scratch. I
turn to you now the you
a house where we are
holders that see but are not there
there the tree does not know us
and we are looking for her old house
we pictured like a black hawk
we don't know how to call
differently than the wind
we cannot live on that
narrator thinking cause is caused
and no other way to consider
forests being said and
saying look, and looking, looking at the
forest now, what do you see now
isn't it different now.

WHEN OBSERVING AN EMBRACE IN THE WOODS WHERE

there there
there are people
we can choose
not to trust
the view
proving worrywoods

what went wrong and how
the last days
findings are needed
mornings when work
does not come
I cannot think of what the woodsmen did

at the edge
but measure figures
the site it is trying
to make you think this
here the least probable
conclusion knowing not this

mistake that the windows
wait name the wall the want
when gated off to know to not
name it at all not want to
name it you should
know you are able to be there

calling for passage
a family is not a falling a
a not owed an owned land
who owes the errors who used to
cover and grow the broken because
because the guard lost

the will to last
and without it
not much else

ONE THING HAS TO FALL AFTER ANOTHER

that you is always you
in the plural may account for
the ill-trained hunters, their fears
of the headless horses
no the leveled forest
is not like I thought
no one is announcing the tiny deer
what to see there
to say about the stolen
saying it was their people
who suffered more
resembling the telling
that you remember
as a possible reason
to respond in detail to their
testimony where we decided
to invent the other— it was there
in the news today: how the worst
silences were taking their time

THINKING IT'S OK TO DISCUSS

This— The best tree

Is sick now, now discuss

Where to look, discuss:

The cause, and, if

Possible, discuss who

Could have prevented

The workers who are working

To prevent, and if it happens then

Prepares to discuss how bodger will

Recognize people saying "sick"

Everywhere, discuss how to handle

Discussing one sickness as if

That sickness is the other

Sickness— A discussion of the landscape

When it changes from woods

To sorry. To not the ideal

Tree to use as the marker

Beginning a discussion by a river

May confuse explanation with justification,

And, how to avoid, when I say I need

A new chair to work, you think:

I am using the chair as a metaphor

SORRY LET IN THE DOOR AND DONE NOTHING SINCE THEN

Copying the agreement over
Onto the meeting table still

Covered in their
Crumbs. Carrying on— It is still
The wolf. The wolf
Crying is his fruit tree growing

Where
I have imagined no

Thinking of the bodger asking the site at dawn
Like a juror

Who cannot finish his job to think
About the fruit falling like

The doormaker at his doorframe thinking
How the neighbor looks

To be playing dead. Say the rooms
Here are too large to stand in

For coffins, the thundering, fear of the soil

Turning— Think of it

Spoiling the door's
Plan. The sad parents,

Waiting to hold wolvesfruits
Where there is a conclusion

That is: the walls go up before the foundation, a
Letter attaches at his feet

It is silenced here. The building is a bark. Is

Chasing. Forget the worrier
Walking into the bodger's position

Where a machine is being made
To make enough room

WHEN THEY REPLICATE THE PROCESS

It is feeling like the waiting room
What is happening in the waiting
Room. That he asks, what do you call

A disruption? Names each stutter by naming
The breaking from the place
Without feeling guilty

Look out the window find the barn

You've always looked at now too large
To be placed in the woods. That you know
To stay focused on the plot

It is always about to
Bring us through. Where us named and known us there
Is no such thing as too much research.

Different views of pith. Cry at this point
You're not a part of the war. This is the war I forgot
To tell you about the copies. They are here.

WOOD CAN HOLD THE WOODEN DOORS IN PLACE

So they can open— Can choose a woods of one tree
A tree carried in a carving

No matter what
Woods are being cut

We have our own private trees
To diagnose the tree before speaking

Do not confuse yourselves with them
They are the they that know you

Set out to convince, not explain.
They welcome the opportunity to talk about loss
This is a way of dividing

Into different forests
Wonder who would challenge that proposition

Call it an event of some trees

Notice in both cases
The scene is a motivator

It's not a performance, it's the expectation
Something is happening in the sentence

We are both looking at it together
Reproducing the thing I don't want you to do

We will be getting there
We are getting there

We are almost there
We are talking about duration, sorry

Sorry, I just have one question
Is that what they meant?

THERE WERE MANY MORE CARPENTERS THEN

All the good woods were going towards ship building

Care for the miniature box was like the entire home

Like a large city's best museum, they changed

What they mean by: figure is looking for the pattern

When constructing an inlay, the number of ways the wood

Can be cut, glued, arranged and re-cut may mean a figure

May be found before fixing the grain to pine for strength

To know where the woods naturally grew helps to see

The place where a piece was made

It's a carpenter's holiday. A house full of paper,

A book called *A Carpenter's Holiday* you did not write

Woods chosen for their best use not their appearance

There is more than one way to write about this tree

If you are aware of the evidence

How legs of a certain wood turn well

The furniture surface changed after the wood burning fires outside

The coal fires caused change, too

Woods are still not the same as plywoods

Though parts of the tree are being used

Many pieces you've said are other woods

Have turned out to be birch

This is a joiner's yard

I was asked to advance

Our craft— To keep approaching the defects

In the woods and to cut them out—

Fill them with patches of wood shaped like boats

To ship the woods from overseas, rather than

To find a neighborhood timber

At least there are woods there

HOW TO FIND THE WOODS

How to say: thanks for inviting me
To think, about our neighbor named for the river

That goes from where you thought about them
To the place we have thought about together

That makes me think of how there isn't an equivalent
In the woods. To the woods

Where a woodsman loses
His voice before getting proper

Directions for how to find another
Plan to show them how

You can prevent the forest
Fire can run away and not fight it

I think there is an I
In that there it is

To stop to read
To now be working like a horse

The time in which it is possible to work
To think about should be

Being our own. Gasps are
The woods' grains

To think about maintaining
Our surfaces, keep on

Finishing with the hand
Where the tools left off

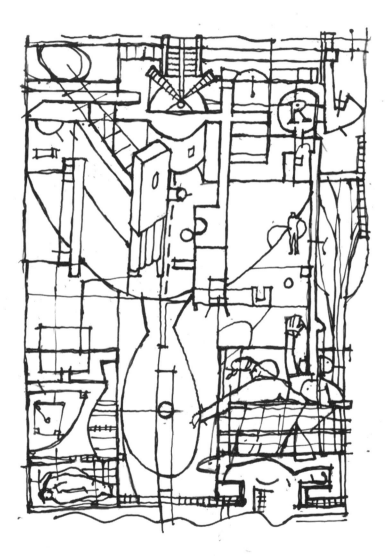

NOTES

"The necessity of a line or a work to be as woods is, to be as clean as wood is as it issues from the hand of nature, to be as shaped as wood can be when a man has had his hand to it."
is from Charles Olson's "Projective Verse."

"—You've got to be careful in woods"
is from Louis Zukofsky's "*A*"-12.

"The leaves are falling. Point things out.
Pick up the right things."
is from Bob Perelman's poem "China" published in *Primer* (This Press 1981).

"Stop! I did not drag my father beyond this tree."
is from Gertrude Stein's *The Making of Americans*.

"In The Seven Woods" takes its title from a page in Susan Howe's *The Midnight* (New Directions 2003). Howe includes the title page of W.B. Yeats's *In the Seven Woods*.

"A Thought The Same As The Bough" takes its title from Louis Zukofsky's "*A*"-12. "Trees grow / symbolic only if you let them" is from a poem I heard Bin Ramke read.

"Will Go North Through Woods To The Wood" takes its title from a line in Susan Howe's *Europe of Trusts* (New Directions 1990).

"The Difficulty of Describing Trees" takes its title from Robert Hass's poem "The Problem of Describing Trees" in *Time and Materials* (Harper Collins 2007).

In the poem "Wood Can Hold The Wooden Doors In Place," "We have our own private trees" is from a poem I heard Matthew Zapruder read and "To the event of some trees" is from a poem I heard Lisa Robertson read.

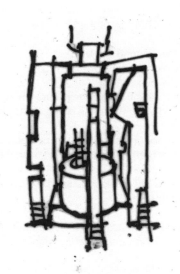

ACKNOWLEDGEMENTS

Many poems appeared in the chapbook *NO, I WILL BE IN THE WOODS* published by E. B. Goodale and Brian Foley's Brave Men Press.

Parts of the poems called "The Plans Caution" appeared in *The Plans Caution*, co-authored with my father, Richard Taransky, published by Andrew Rippeon's QUEUE books.

Thank you to the generous editors, publishers, and readers of: *jubilat, glitter pony, Jerry Magazine, 20012, Bone Bouquet, VOLT, Apiary, milk magazine, We Are Happy To Know Something, The Offending Adam, Invisible Ear, Sprung Formal, Wunderkammer,* "Poem-A-Day" from *The Academy of American Poets, Lungfull!, Big Bridge, Rabbit Light Movies, Wolf In A Field, Staging Ground,* and *The Huffington Post*, where poems from *Sorry Was In The Woods* were published.

MORE ABOUT THE AUTHOR

Michelle Taransky's first book, *Barn Burned, Then* was selected by Marjorie Welish for the 2008 Omnidawn Poetry Prize. A graduate of The University of Chicago and The Iowa Writers' Workshop, Taransky lives in Philadelphia and is a member of the Critical Writing Faculty at University of Pennsylvania and Reviews Editor for *Jacket2*.

Sorry Was In The Woods
by Michelle Taransky

Cover text set in Birch Std and Copperplate Gothic Std
Interior text set in Myriad Pro

Cover art:
"Civil Settlement" by Richard Taransky, FAAR '00,
Artist in Residence '05 with The Fabric Workshop and Museum,
Philadelphia, PA.

Interior images by Richard Taransky:
"Bath House" "Bride's House" "Cinema"
"City Gate" "Exit Section" "Grand Stands" "House"

Cover and interior design by Cassandra Smith

Omnidawn Publishing
Richmond, California
2013

Ken Keegan & Rusty Morrison, Co-Publishers & Senior Editors
Cassandra Smith, Poetry Editor & Book Designer
Gillian Hamel, Poetry Editor & OmniVerse Managing Editor
Sara Mumolo, Poetry Editor
Peter Burghardt, Poetry Editor & Book Designer
Turner Canty, Poetry Editor
Juliana Paslay, Fiction Editor & Bookstore Outreach Manager
Liza Flum, Poetry Editor & Social Media
Sharon Osmond, Poetry Editor & Bookstore Outreach
Gail Aronson, Fiction Editor
RJ Ingram, Social Media
Craig Santos Perez, Media Consultant